WHEN CHRIST CALLS

WHEN CHRIST CALLS

John W. Whitehead

TRI PRESS®

Charlottesville, VA

When Christ Calls

© 2006 by Glass Onion Productions

Printed in the United States of America by TRI PRESS®

For information, contact:
TRI PRESS
Post Office Box 7482
Charlottesville, VA 22906-7482

ISBN: 0-9772331-3-8

Scripture quotations are taken from the
New King James Version.

Book design by Chris Combs

This book is a tribute to the spirit of faith that compelled Dietrich Bonhoeffer, and others like him, to stand against oppression and persecution.

It is the same spirit that I see lived out every day, in untold ways, in the men, women and children of all ages and from all walks of life who willingly put their lives and their livelihoods on the line to answer Christ's call.

If we can learn one thing from these courageous Christians, it should be what it means to follow Christ.

Try to exclude the possibility of suffering which the order of nature and the existence of free wills involve, and you find that you have excluded life itself.

—C. S. Lewis

CONTENTS

ACKNOWLEDGMENTS

This book centers on our obligation to help one another, no matter the cost. Throughout my life, I have been blessed by many who have enabled me to persevere. I appreciate the editing and research of Nisha Mohammed and Carol Whitehead. Rita Dunaway's research assistance was invaluable. Also, thanks to Mike and Patrice Masters, Tom and Judy Neuberger and Jim Knicely for their many years of support and encouragement. Without these people, and friends like them, I could not have written the following words.

CHAPTER ONE

The Price

When Christ calls a man, he bids him come and die.
> —Dietrich Bonhoeffer

Dietrich Bonhoeffer is one of the 20th century's greatest examples of someone who, when faced with evil, struggled to come to grips with what Christ would have him do. And it is this struggle that is presented in his seminal work, *The Cost of Discipleship*.

Taking a stand for one's faith is rarely easy. There is always a price to be paid, whether it be a loss of life, livelihood or constant persecution. Having fought on the front lines for religious freedom for the past 25 years, I have come to a first-hand understanding of what it means to take up one's cross and follow Christ. What I have learned is that although it is not necessary to be a Bonhoeffer in order to answer Christ's call, there is much that can be learned from his struggle to stand and serve.

Answering Christ's call is not reserved for the foot soldiers and the martyrs of the faith. It is a call to every man, woman and child to stand for justice, to show compassion, to share Christ's love and to do God's work. It is a call that comes to each and every one of us at some point in our lives. For some, it is a call to serve those in need.

For others, it is a call to stand and fight. For still others, it is a call to sacrificially support those on the front lines. For Bonhoeffer, it was all of the aforementioned and one thing more: a call to die to his own ambitions and dreams in order to serve Christ and, in so doing, find life in Christ.

There is no protocol to follow for answering when Christ calls. However, there are certain elements common to the struggles that often precede answering Christ's call.

First, like Bonhoeffer, you must deny your own personal ambitions and needs. In other words, you must die to Self.

Second, you must understand the nature of Christ. He was a radical, a revolutionary who was controversial in His time. How much more so would He be in our day?

Third, be willing to be controversial and revolutionary, as was Christ.

Fourth, recognize that evil exists. We cannot turn a blind eye to what is troubling, ugly or unjust. There is a tendency in all of us to turn aside or change the channel when confronted with images of starvation, death and suffering.

Loath to leave our comfort zones, we choose instead to turn our eyes away. But the first step in doing is seeing.

Fifth, you must consider what will happen to those who are suffering if you do nothing. As Edmund Burke said, "All it takes for evil to triumph is for good men to do nothing."

Sixth, be like Christ practically and spiritually. The theology of happiness touted by some leading televangelists of our day is not Christ-like theology. Christ does not call us to be happy; He calls us to serve by taking up our crosses and following Him.

Seventh, recognize that it will not be easy. Suffering is inevitable.

Eighth, deny yourself, take up your cross and follow Him, all the while knowing that there is always a price to pay.

And, finally, you must act. You must speak truth to power, recognizing that doing so will mean putting everything of this world behind you in order to put Christ first. You must live out Christ's commandments to love God and your neighbor.

CHAPTER TWO

Come and Die

It is not the religious act that makes the Christian, but the participation in the suffering of God in the world.
—Dietrich Bonhoeffer

Share the trials and the suffering. Refuse to remain silent. Stand and fight. These three ideals shaped much of Dietrich Bonhoeffer's life and led to his eventual death at the hands of the Nazis. Yet before anything else could happen, Bonhoeffer had to choose between a life of security and a life of suffering. His faith in Jesus Christ determined the road he would follow.

A man of great moral courage and conviction, Bonhoeffer refused to remain silent about a world filled with war, torture and other atrocities. Willing to make the ultimate sacrifice for his beliefs, he felt morally compelled to speak out and openly protest. Were he alive today, he would undoubtedly be appalled at the absence of outrage on the part of most of the Christian community to the evils of our day.

Bonhoeffer, a pastor and theologian, was no stranger to taking a moral stand against what was popular, powerful and accepted. He spent much of his adult life urging the German church to resist Nazism. And when he could not prevail upon the church to interfere in political matters, he took action. In fact, it was Bonhoeffer's involvement in a plot to kill Adolf Hitler that resulted in his execution on April 9, 1945. He was only 39 years old.

Bonhoeffer's theologically rooted opposition to Nazism led him to become a Christian dissident and an advocate on behalf of German Jews. It was his efforts to help a group of Jews escape to Switzerland that led to his arrest and imprisonment in the spring of 1943. Bonhoeffer's thoughts and writings provide a rare insight into his strength of religious conviction and willingness to act on principle, no matter the cost.

Although he fought the Nazis, Bonhoeffer was also sharply critical of Christianity. He believed that Christians, much like many evangelicals today, compartmentalized their faith so that it affected only certain areas of their lives. In the process, they were self-absorbed, looking only to their own spiritual and material well-being. Bonhoeffer berated the church for such self-absorption. "We are otherworldly—ever since we hit upon the devious trick of being religious, yes even 'Christian' at the expense of the earth," he wrote in 1932.

As the influence of Nazism grew in Germany, Bonhoeffer, a Lutheran, urged the Lutheran Church to fight it. After the first anti-Semitic laws took effect, he outlined a progression of steps that the church must take against oppressive government. First, the church must speak out against abuses of power. Second, the church must aid victims of such abuses. Finally, when other measures fail, the church must take direct action against the government.

In 1933, ignoring the protests of Bonhoeffer and other dissenting pastors, the Lutheran Church adopted a set of Aryan clauses—non-Aryans and those married to non-Aryans were no longer to be ordained or offered positions in the church. Bonhoeffer immediately called for all dissenting pastors to resign and even refused the parish that had been offered to him. He also sent a statement to church leaders declaring that the Aryan clauses were in direct conflict with basic Christian doctrines. When he received no response, Bonhoeffer helped form the Pastors' Emergency League, which eventually grew to 6,000 dissenting pastors.

Even within the rebel church, Bonhoeffer was considered something of a radical. And his stand against Hitler's war machine separated him from his fellow pastors, many of whom backed some of Hitler's policies and movement toward war. Though he considered the church to be Christ's primary agent for change in the world, Bonhoeffer did not hesitate to act independently when he deemed it necessary. He lived his convictions through personal, and usually very practical, acts of dissent.

Out of expedience, Bonhoeffer carried out many of his anti-Nazi activities in secret (including avoiding military service). At the height of Nazi power, to publicly attack Hitler meant prison or death. Bonhoeffer knew he could be more effective if he were not perceived as a threat.

When the Nazi government began taking Jewish lives, Bonhoeffer resorted to even more covert tactics. He helped arrange a successful scheme to smuggle a group of Jews out of Germany. He also came to the aid of the mentally and physically handicapped who were slated to be euthanized. Bonhoeffer and his father, who headed the Department of Psychology at the University of Berlin, obtained evidence from medical experts to support their refusal to hand over patients housed at two church-run facilities.

In 1939, Bonhoeffer traveled to America with the intention of waiting out the war. He soon realized, however, that he could not in good conscience desert his fellow Germans. Incredibly, he returned to Germany, knowing that this would place his life in imminent danger. After his return, Bonhoeffer became actively involved in plans for a military coup.

The plans for a military coup, however, suffered a setback when, in December 1941, Hitler made himself commander-in-chief of the German army. Conspiracy leaders then determined that the coup would have to begin with an assassination, and Bonhoeffer found himself a party to plans to murder Hitler. As he explained, "If I see a madman driving a car into a group of innocent bystanders, then I can't, as a Christian, simply wait for the catastrophe and then comfort the wounded and bury the dead. I must try to wrestle the steering wheel out of the hands of the driver."

Eventually, one of Bonhoeffer's co-conspirators was arrested by the Nazis and he, in turn, implicated Bonhoeffer. Bonhoeffer was arrested by the Gestapo on April 5, 1943, but the conspiracy continued to move forward. Two attempts to kill Hitler had already failed, and on July 20, 1944, Bonhoeffer learned that the third and final attempt on Hitler's life had also failed. In the days following, Hitler ordered a series of executions of those involved in the assassination plot.

At this point, Bonhoeffer's prison guard was willing to help him escape, and an elaborate plan was set in motion. But as more and more people were arrested for the slightest connection to the conspirators, Bonhoeffer decided that his escape would amount to an admission of guilt and endanger his family and friends.

The conspiracy was widespread, and Hitler had some 6,000 executed in retaliation. But since Bonhoeffer was considered a possible source of information, he was kept alive for several months. Hitler only ordered his execution after

Germany's defeat became inevitable.

Bonhoeffer went calmly to his death. As he was led from his cell, he was observed by the prison doctor, who said: "Through the half-open door I saw Pastor Bonhoeffer still in his prison clothes, kneeling in fervent prayer to the Lord his God. The devotion and evident conviction of being heard that I saw in the prayer of this intensely captivating man moved me to the depths." The prisoners were then ordered to strip. Naked under the scaffold, Bonhoeffer knelt one last time to pray. Five minutes later, he was dead.

Bonhoeffer was hanged at the Flossenbürg Concentration Camp on April 9, 1945. A few days later, Allied troops reached and liberated the camp. On April 30, Adolf Hitler committed suicide. On May 7, Germany surrendered unconditionally.

For Bonhoeffer, the cost of discipleship was isolation, imprisonment and ultimately death. He remains a model of the Christian struggle to do the right thing versus taking the path of least resistance.

CHAPTER THREE

Turn the World Upside Down

These who have turned the world upside down have come here too.

—Acts 17:6

Hopefully all Christians would agree that they are called to emulate Jesus Christ. Why, then, are so many bent on pursuing their own success and happiness? Would Jesus be considered successful or happy by modern American standards? Surely not.

He was an itinerant preacher. He acquired no wealth or possessions. He didn't even have a home of His own, as far as we know. He kept company with those who would have been considered the dregs of humanity—prostitutes, tax collectors and sick people. And during His lifetime, at least, His ministry must have been seen by the watching world as a failure. In modern terms, He would have been considered a loser. The self-proclaimed "King of the Jews" was rejected by His contemporaries. The most religious among them—who might have been expected to recognize and follow Him most quickly—instead repeatedly questioned His authority and even His identity.

Jesus had to constantly be on the move to evade the teams of men setting traps for Him, trying to assassinate Him, crush His following and give Him the same treatment given the beheaded John the Baptist. He had to go into hiding. He was in constant danger of being kidnapped, arrested, assassinated, stoned for His "irreligion" or thrown off a cliff. Likewise, Herod Antipas, who killed John the Baptist openly, plotted to kill Jesus secretly. As Gary Wills points out in his book *What Christ Meant*: "For two years, Jesus slipped through all the traps set for him. He moved like a fish in the sea of his lower-class fellows. He kept on the move, in the countryside."

Just as many of us misunderstand our purpose in life, the religious leaders of the day misunderstood Christ's purpose in life. They were expecting a powerful Messiah and could not accept a humble one. They were expecting a world leader. They could not accept a servant who washed the dirty feet of men or who entered Jerusalem riding a donkey. They were looking for a rule-follower. They could not accept this humble rabbi who valued simple faith over the keeping of legalistic traditions.

With the benefit of hindsight and a lifetime

of indoctrination, it's easy for us to look down on the Pharisees and wonder, "How could they have missed it so badly?" But the reason the Pharisees "missed it" is the same reason so many of us miss it. It is because Christ's message, in its purest form, is offensive, hard to swallow and, in many instances, incredibly difficult to follow. While the religious leaders of Jesus' time simply rejected Him and His offensive message, we modern-day Christians often try to accept Jesus by changing His message. We soften it up just enough so that it won't be too intimidating or beyond our reach.

And, sadly, modern Christendom softens the image of Christ and presents Him as a meek, harmless friend of the world. However, that is not the picture found in the Bible. Far from being passive and meek, Jesus Christ was both contro-versial and dogmatic.

Jesus challenged the belief system of the society of His day. He turned everything upside down. For example, Christ taught that what is valued in the kingdom of heaven is not material prosperity but poverty of spirit and mercy. This is all set forth in the Sermon on the Mount.

When did you last read the Sermon on the Mount? Did the Beatitudes strike you as incredible, almost incomprehensible and nearly humanly impossible to consistently practice? If not, you should read them again. In Philip Yancey's book *The Jesus I Never Knew*, he tells a story about a friend of his, a professor, who assigned the Sermon on the Mount to her composition class at Texas A&M University. She asked the students to write a short essay about it, and these are a couple of their responses:

> "The stuff the churches preach is extremely strict and allows for almost no fun without thinking it is a sin."

> "I did not like the essay 'Sermon on the Mount.' It was hard to read and made me feel like I had to be perfect, and no one is."

Rather than being outraged or disappointed by these responses, the professor was encouraged. She found it refreshing to encounter mainstream Americans who had not heard the Beatitudes so many times that they became unremarkable.

Jesus' message runs counter to the rampant materialism that dominates our society and, too often, our churches. It declares that all our wealth and power are of absolutely no eternal value. What's more, it declares that all our best efforts "to be good enough for God" are like filthy rags to Him.

Imagine how you would have received the Sermon on the Mount if you had been there. You would have been weary from the oppressive rule of the Romans and longing for a Messiah who would come with great power, set you free from the miseries of your life and make you happy. Instead, Jesus tells you to turn the other cheek and assures you that for all the suffering you endure, you are "blessed."

Unfortunately, most of us have become inoculated to the heart of Christ's message. Unable to find a way of reconciling this reversal of our worldly values, we find a way to gloss over Christ's teaching or think of it as merely philosophical, with no practical application to our lives.

But when we take an honest look at the Jesus we find in the Gospels, who, we recall, is God in the flesh, what we find is no mild-mannered, nice, go-with-the-flow sort of person. Instead, we find someone who would surely be seen by today's Christian population as a rebel, a radical and even an outcast.

Francis Schaeffer, in his book *The Church at the End of the Twentieth Century*, recognized the revolutionary nature of Christ's teaching, while at the same time the modern church's tendency to identify with the establishment, or our politically driven, materialistic society:

> The danger is that the evangelical, being so committed to middle-class norms and often even elevating these norms to an equal place with God's absolutes, will slide without thought into accepting some form of an establishment elite.

What will happen to the church in that situation?

Schaeffer explains:

> Certainly, at least at first, an establish-
> ment elite will be less harsh on the
> church than a left-wing elite if that
> should come into power. But that is a
> danger. The church will tend to make
> peace with the establishment and identify
> itself with it. It will seem better at first,
> but not in the end.

This identification of Christians with the
establishment elite has been magnified in recent
years with the overt involvement of the church in
conservative politics. That is why Schaeffer
warned:

> One of the greatest injustices we do to our
> young people is to ask them to be conser-
> vative. Christianity today is not conserva-
> tive, but revolutionary. To be conservative
> today is to miss the whole point, for con-
> servatism means standing in the flow of
> the status quo…. If we want to be fair, we

must teach the young to be revolutionaries, revolutionaries against the status quo.

The teachings of Christ undermined the political and religious establishment of His day—especially the religious establishment, which was built upon legalism, wealth and self-righteousness. He overturned the money changers' tables in the Temple. Jesus rebuked the proud, self-righteous religious snobs and instead chose as His disciples the humble, uneducated men who could readily see their need of Him.

Jesus was a revolutionary. So how can we call ourselves His disciples if we are content to simply fit in and go about life seeking our own self-fulfillment and accumulating wealth? Our purpose in life should not be success, happiness or even personal peace. Our purpose in life is to follow the call of Christ, our Lord. Indeed, the very title "Lord" presupposes that its bearer is one to whom service and obedience are due. We have no right to call Jesus "Lord" unless we are in a place of submission to His call.

But what does Jesus call us to do? Let me

point you to His own words in Mark 8:34-36: "Whoever desires to come after Me, let him deny himself, and take up his cross, and follow Me. For whoever desires to save his life will lose it, but whoever loses his life for My sake and the gospel's will save it. For what will it profit a man if he gains the whole world, and loses his own soul?"

As theologian John R.W. Stott explains in his classic book *Christ the Controversialist*, true Christianity is inevitably and "essentially dogmatic." Why? As Stott writes, "It purports to be a revealed faith." He continues:

> If the Christian religion were just a collection of the philosophical and ethical ideas of men (like Hinduism), dogmatism would be entirely out of place. But if God has spoken (as Christians claim), both in olden days through the prophets and in these last days through His Son, why should it be thought "dogmatic" to believe His Word ourselves and to urge other people to believe it too?

Stott adds that Jesus Christ was not "broad-minded" in the popular sense of the word. He was not prepared to accept as valid all views on every subject. Jesus Christ was not afraid to dissent from official doctrines that He knew to be wrong (or not "politically correct"). He was not afraid to expose error or speak truth to power. He called false teachers "blind guides," "wolves in sheep's clothing," "whitewashed tombs" and even "a brood of vipers."

Christ was literally on the offensive, with a message that offended those around Him to the point that they killed him. One illustration, found in Matthew 21, describes Christ's action in the Temple: "Then Jesus went into the temple of God and drove out all those who bought and sold in the temple, and overturned the tables of the money changers and the seats of those who sold doves." Christ pointed out that the Temple should be "a house of prayer" but that it had been made into "a den of thieves."

In addition, Christ would not permit anyone to carry goods through the Temple and even blocked the doorways. In short, He took the

Truth to the world and commanded His disciples to do likewise:

> And Jesus came and spoke to them, saying, "All authority has been given to Me in heaven and on earth. Go therefore and make disciples of all the nations, baptizing them in the name of the Father and of the Son and of the Holy Spirit, teaching them to observe all things that I have commanded you; and lo, I am with you always, *even* to the end of the age."

Jesus was also called an agent of the devil or the devil himself. He was considered unclean and a consorter with Samaritans and immoral women. He was accused of promoting immorality, of being a glutton and drunkard and a mocker of the Jewish law. In either ancient or modern terms, He could never be considered respectable. In fact, He shocked the elders and priests of the Temple when He said: "Assuredly, I say to you that tax collectors and harlots enter the kingdom of God before you."

The early Christians took Christ's teachings and example with the utmost seriousness. Stott writes:

> The apostles also were controversialists, as is plain from the New Testament Epistles, and they appealed to their readers "to contend for the faith which was once for all delivered to the saints." Like their Lord and master they found it necessary to warn the churches of false teachers and urge them to stand firm in the truth.

There are many examples of confrontation and controversy in the New Testament. For example, the Apostle Paul preached in a Jewish synagogue in Thessalonica, with the result that some came to believe what he was saying. However, those who opposed Paul formed a mob and incited a riot. In this case, the mere preaching of the truth caused the confrontation. The apostles would hardly have been described as men who "turned the world upside down," as the

King James Version puts it in Acts 17, if they had casually explained the truth or allowed other points of view to be taken on an equal basis. Truth and confrontation often go hand in hand.

Controversy, it should be stressed, flows from the collision of truth with falsehood. Controversy, however, should not result from the *manner* in which the truth is presented. In other words, in a confrontational situation, controversy should be a result of the message, not the messenger. For example, when the Gospels note that the Scribes and Pharisees were plotting to kill Jesus Christ, they give the reason: "For they feared Him, because all the people were astonished at His *teaching*."

Many Christians, however, shy away from any form of confrontation. And many pastors and churches seek to "fit in" in hopes of making Christ more palatable to a modern pluralistic society that often values materialism over all things.

Why do we do this? As human beings, we naturally want to seek our own comfort, pleasure and success. We value strength, health and power and look down upon weakness, suffering and submission. And we don't want to face the fact that practicing what Christ taught will often create problems and make us uncomfortable.

However, in a world that is seething with evil, we cannot afford to selfishly pursue our pleasures and comforts. To practice true Christianity, we have to be willing to recognize and challenge untruth. And above all, much like Dietrich Bonhoeffer, we must be willing to sacrifice our most prized possessions—and our lives if necessary—to serve Christ.

CHAPTER FOUR

Recognize That Evil Exists

Be sober, be vigilant; because your adversary the devil walks about like a roaring lion, seeking whom he may devour.

—I Peter 5:8

The repertoire of evil has never been richer than it is today. "Yet never have our responses been so weak," writes Professor Andrew Delbanco in his insightful book *The Death of Satan: How Americans Have Lost the Sense of Evil.*

We are bombarded by chaotic and murderously destructive images on a daily basis, but we have lost a way to articulate the nature of the evil that we see. Thus, when met with a shocking new cruelty, most Americans, anxious and amazed, simply shudder, wince and then switch the channel. It is easier to escape into entertainment and other distractions, rather than face reality.

Serial killers and rapists; school shootings where children and teachers are murdered; corporate thievery and greed; terrorists murdering thousands of innocent people—there must be a better explanation for these acts of violence than the simple and oft-resorted-to belief that the perpetrators hate us, for whatever reason. In fact, centuries ago evil had a name, a face and an explanation, and it was grounded in our Judeo-

Christian beliefs. As Delbanco writes, "It was called the Fall, it was personified by the devil, and it was attributed to an original sin committed in Eden and imputed by God to all mankind."

For much of the history of Western civilization, Satan was a presence in most people's lives. He was a symbol and an explanation for both the cruelties one received and those perpetrated upon others. That concept has since been lost to a modern society steeped in the deadening embrace of science and materialism. Consequently, we are left without the moral markers we once depended on for knowing who, and where, we are.

Whatever position one takes on the question of evil, there was once a concept of sin. It may have been broad and somewhat capricious, but it was meaningful. And it has now faded into a sea of moral ambiguity. As Lionel Tiger writes in *The Manufacture of Evil*: "Once upon a time, evil was personified. Evil was Mephistopheles or the Devil. Almost flavorful, altogether identifiable, a clarified being from another world."

Most Americans, for example, once believed

the world to be an emanation of the mind of God. And anything that happened in it—be it war, famine, pestilence—had punitive or admonitory meaning. As late as 1912, when the "unsinkable" Titanic sank on its maiden voyage, the press coverage of the disaster recounted it as a "lesson written in searing lines on ice-floe and curling wave-crest." The lesson was scriptural and was most likely taken from Christ's statement in Luke 14:11: "For whoever exalts himself will be abased, and he who humbles himself will be exalted." Today, however, the world for most people is regarded as a place of unknown origin in which we find ourselves adrift for no known reason.

Unfortunately, "as we lose touch with the idea of evil," Delbanco writes, "we seem to need more and more vivid representations of it—as if it were a drug whose potency diminishes with each use." The vivid images out of horror films and books and the steady diet of death images on the never-ending news programs attest to this.

No matter how repugnant the idea of an evil being that corrupts our institutions and causes horrible catastrophes may be, most people, if they are honest with themselves, will admit that they yearn for a world in which what they see happening can be explained. They cling to the idea of a world where responsibility for evil is clear, whether it be a supernatural force or the evil that somehow resides within each of us and is manipulated by that force or entity. They find comfort in a world where evil can still be recognized, have meaning and require a response.

Our flustered response to evil and the being that represents it is cogently summed up in Thomas Harris' horror novel *The Silence of the Lambs* in an exchange between Hannibal Lecter, a psychiatrist who bites his victims to death and then cannibalizes them, and the young female FBI agent who seeks his help in pursuing another serial killer. Peering from within his plexiglass prison, the madman poses the modern dilemma:

> Nothing happened to me, Officer Starling. I happened. You can't reduce me to a set of influences. You've given up good and evil for behaviorism, Officer

Starling. You've got everybody in moral dignity pants—nothing is ever anybody's fault. Look at me, Officer Starling. Can you stand to say I'm evil?

What is terrifying is not so much what the monster Lecter says. The horror is that we cannot seem to answer his question.

In his book *Knowing God*, author J. I. Packer aptly explains the troubling phenomenon we currently face as "the doctrine of a celestial Santa Claus," which is characterized by a "certainty that there is no more to be said of God…than that he is infinitely forbearing and kind." Packer explains that once this doctrine has put down roots, true Christianity simply dies off. This is because, under the Santa Claus theory, sins create no problem and atonement of sins through Christ's suffering on the cross becomes unnecessary. For followers of this doctrine, "God's active favor extends no less to those who disregard his commands than to those who keep them."

Packer goes on to explain that the Santa

Claus theology "carries within itself the seeds of its own collapse, for it cannot cope with the fact of evil." The world is full of evil, and bad things happen to good people. Pain is an inevitable consequence of life. But this should not weaken our faith in God. Rather, it should give us hope in the midst of hardship.

Christians serve a God who is vast, wise and holy. But in His love for us, He allows us to encounter hardships and unhappiness. He allows us to *suffer*, just as He allowed His own Son to suffer. In fact, He *calls* us to suffer in our following of Christ.

Although he had many opportunities to turn aside from the trouble brewing in Germany, Dietrich Bonhoeffer recognized the evil at work within the Nazi regime and heeded Christ's call to stand against it. He did not presume to choose his own happiness or well-being—or even that of those he loved most in this world—over God's call to suffering. One memoir of Bonhoeffer's life recounts how "in his hearing before the Gestapo during his imprisonment, defenseless and powerless as he then was and only fortified by the word of God in his heart, he stood erect and unbroken before his tormentors. He refused to recant… although he was continually threatened with torture and with the arrest of his parents, his sisters and his fiancée." Here was a man who valued God above all else and had determined to be a disciple of Christ at any cost.

CHAPTER FIVE

What Will Happen to Them?

So which of these three do you think was neighbor to him who fell among the thieves? And he said, "He who showed mercy on him." Then Jesus said to him, "Go and do likewise."
—Christ

What would drive a man to voluntarily return to a country where he knew death awaited him? Who would refuse a chance to escape the hangman's noose and instead place himself in death's way? Who would break the law and risk capture to smuggle others to safety?

The answer is that rare person who knows what it means to truly follow Christ—and a person who knows what it is to be selfless. Dietrich Bonhoeffer was such a person.

We need this same kind of radical unselfishness in the modern church—a focus on a non-self-centered otherness. This is the same spirit that motivated Bonhoeffer and the same unselfishness that moved the Samaritan in Luke 10 to act.

Although most of us know the story of the Good Samaritan, it is worth repeating.

One day a man came to Jesus. This man, a lawyer, wanted to raise some questions about vital matters in life. Among other things, he asked Jesus "Who is my neighbor?" From the way the lawyer phrased his questions, it was clear that he was trying to trick Jesus. He wanted to show Jesus that he knew a little more than Christ knew and, through this, throw Jesus off-base. The questions could have easily ended up in a philosophical and theological debate.

The Reverend Martin Luther King, Jr. often found himself in a similar thicket of questions and controversy. On April 3, 1968, the day before he was assassinated, King was in Memphis to help striking sanitation workers get a fair wage. The night before, he spoke to a church audience in Memphis about Christ's dilemma and the questions as posed by the lawyer:

> Jesus immediately pulled that question from mid-air, and placed it on a danger-ous curve between Jerusalem and Jericho. And he talked about a certain man, who fell among thieves. You remember that a Levite and a priest passed by on the other side. They didn't stop to help him. And finally a man of another race came by. He got down from his beast, decided not to be compassion-

ate by proxy. But with him, administered first aid, and helped the man in need. Jesus ended up saying, this was the good man, this was the great man, because he had the capacity to project the "I" into the "thou," and to be concerned about his brother.

In our hectic, chaotic lives, it is easy to imagine how the average person, even one wishing to live a life devoted to Christ, can become distracted. And sometimes the often endless stream of church meetings, as Dr. King notes, could very well deter us from helping someone who has fallen by the wayside:

Now you know, we use our imagination a great deal to try to determine why the priest and the Levite didn't stop. At times we say they were busy going to church meetings—an ecclesiastical gathering—and they had to get on down to Jerusalem so they wouldn't be late for their meeting.

Or maybe the religious rules, which some refer to as legalism, by which we live our lives become a deterrent to being a Good Samaritan. But as Dr. King pointed out, there are other reasons that force some not to help:

> But I'm going to tell you what my imagination tells me. It's possible that these men were afraid. You see, the Jericho road is a dangerous road. I remember when Mrs. King and I were first in Jerusalem. We rented a car and drove from Jerusalem down to Jericho. And as soon as we got on that road, I said to my wife, "I can see why Jesus used this as a setting for his parable." It's a winding, meandering road. It's really conducive for ambushing. You start out in Jerusalem, which is about 1200 miles, or rather 1200 feet above sea level. And by the time you get down to Jericho, fifteen or twenty minutes later, you're about 2200 feet below sea level. That's a dangerous road. In the days of Jesus it came to be known as the "Bloody Pass."

Fear is often our greatest enemy. And it is possible that the priest and the Levite looked over at the man on the ground and wondered if the robbers were still lurking nearby. Or it is possible that they believed the man on the ground was faking. In other words, he was merely acting as if he had been robbed and injured in order to lure them close so he could rob them.

One thing is certain. The moment of truth had come. What would they do? Obviously, the first question the Levite asked was, "If I stop to help this man, what will happen to me?"

But the Good Samaritan came by and reversed the question: "If I do not stop to help this man, what will happen to *him*?" That was the question Martin Luther King, Jr. posed to the Christian audience that night:

> That's the question before you tonight. Not, "If I stop to help the sanitation workers, what will happen to all of the hours that I usually spend in my office every day and every week as a pastor?" The question is not, "If I stop to help this

man in need, what will happen to me?"
"If I do not stop to help the sanitation
workers, what will happen to them?"
That's the question.

Not to Please Ourselves

The Apostle Paul in Romans 15:1 likewise
admonishes us: "We then who are strong ought
to bear with the scruples of the weak, and not to
please ourselves." God would, thus, have us to
be Good Samaritans and help those who are
despised and find themselves helpless in our
often chaotic world. Indeed, we are in this world
to help each other. But what does it mean to help
such people? It certainly means more than prayer
or paying lip-service to a need.

But we must be careful not to reduce our
concept of helping to mere emotion. Saddam
Hussein is known to have shed tears for the people he liquidated, and there are observers who
feel his tears were genuine. However, while it is
said that "the devil never sleeps," he does weep.
Thus, if we are to be truly effective in our help-

ing of others, we must have what the Levite and the priest did not possess. As Christ tells us, when the Good Samaritan saw the injured man, "he had *compassion* on him." This means showing concern for another beyond any negative impact it may have on us or our possessions.

This will necessarily mean helping beyond the minimal. In fact, as Christ recognizes in the parable, the Good Samaritan helped this poor man by bandaging his wounds and taking him to a place where he could be cared for. The Good Samaritan even left money for the injured man's care. In other words, he went far out of his way to help a fellow human being who had fallen on bad times. And as Christ tells His disciples, "Go and do likewise."

Christ provides the model for what we should be as compassionate, caring people. In Matthew 22, when Christ was asked which commandment was the most important, He replied:

> "*You shall love the LORD your God with all your heart, with all your soul, and with all your mind.*" This is *the* first and

great commandment. And *the* second *is* like it: "*You shall love your neighbor as yourself.*" On these two commandments hang all the Law and the Prophets.

Christ emphasized dedicating one's *whole self* to serving God by loving our fellow human beings (our neighbors) and treating them with the same measure of love and respect that we believe we deserve. If we strive to accomplish this, we can be of great service to God in accomplishing what any good person should—helping the less fortunate.

Indeed, Christ characterized His own mission in this fashion. In Luke 4, Christ states:

The Spirit of the Lord is upon Me, Because He has anointed Me to preach the gospel to the poor. He has sent Me to heal the brokenhearted, To preach deliverance to the captives And recovery of sight to the blind, To set at liberty those who are oppressed, To preach the acceptable year of the Lord.

As Good Samaritans, we are thus duty-bound to assist those who are oppressed. The "oppressed" include unfortunate souls who are harassed, jailed and even tortured for their beliefs. These, in Christ's terms, are our neighbors. The "oppressed"—our neighbors—also include the economically disadvantaged—the poor and the homeless—who can and should benefit from our attention to their material needs. This means giving to the poor even when it hurts us to give. In other words, what is required is sacrificial giving. As C. S. Lewis writes in *Mere Christianity*:

> I am afraid the only safe rule is to give more than we can spare. In other words, if our expenditure on comforts, luxuries, amusements, etc., is up to the standard common among those with the same income as our own, we are probably giving away too little. If our charities do not at all pinch or hamper us, I should say they are too small. There ought to be things we should like to do and cannot do

because our charitable expenditure excludes them.

The bottom line is that none of us can exist very long without help from other human beings. This is brought home forcefully in a story that Garret Keizer recounts in his book *Help: The Original Human Dilemma*. As Keizer writes, supposedly in hell the damned sit around a great pot, all hungry, because the spoons they hold are too long to bring the food to their mouths. In heaven, people are sitting around the same pot with the same long spoons, but everyone is full. Why? Because in heaven, people use their long spoons to feed one another.

This story reminds me of the ring given to Oscar Schindler by the Jewish workers he had managed to save from the Holocaust. Schindler, who was immortalized in the 1993 film *Schindler's List*, risked his life and lost his fortune in order to help the Jews. The inscription on the ring read: "Whoever saves a single soul saves the entire world."

Of course, this brings us full circle to the

basic question faced by so many fine Christians who went before us, such as Dietrich Bonhoeffer. And it is the same question we face today in a myriad of situations. But we must always, if we are to follow Christ, ask the right one: If I do not stop to help the unfortunate souls around me, what will happen to them?

CHAPTER SIX

Be Like Christ, Practically and Spiritually

No servant can serve two masters; for either he will hate the one and love the other, or else he will be loyal to the one and despise the other. You cannot serve God and mammon.

      —Christ

Even while he was in prison, Bonhoeffer maintained his pastoral role. Those who were with him spoke of the guidance and spiritual inspiration he gave not only to fellow inmates but to prison guards as well. In a letter smuggled out of prison, Bonhoeffer showed no bitterness but rather explained: "We in the resistance have learned to see the great events of world history from below, from the perspective of the excluded, the ill treated, the powerless, the oppressed and despised...so that personal suffering has become a more useful key for understanding the world than personal happiness."

Again, we must ask, what is the secret behind a life like that of Bonhoeffer? Courage? Sheer determination? A great love of others? Selflessness? Those were all traits that Dietrich Bonhoeffer most certainly possessed. But I believe that the more fundamental characteristic which set him apart from the vast majority of people—even other Christians—was his thorough understanding and embracing of his true purpose in life. He knew that his citizenship was not of this world—he was but a pilgrim here on earth.

But what about the vast majority of people? Most work long, hard hours while seldom focusing on anything other than their secular vocation—simply chasing the next big promotion that will land them the next big car or pay for the new addition to their house. By and large, many of us have become materialists and are focused on temporal things—possessions, perfecting our bodily appearance or the personal fulfillment we get from our performance in our career. We have, so to speak, become obsessed with the pursuit of happiness through material possessions—a philosophy that has come to dominate many mainstream churches as well.

Indeed, the concern voiced by some about modern Christianity's seeming ineffectiveness in the face of the rapid moral decline in society and culture may be due to the fact that many who call themselves Christians simply have the wrong focus in life. Our purpose in life is not to be "successful" in this world.

In spending our lives pursuing so-called happiness, just like everyone around us, we put our tent pegs down as deeply as they will go into the sod of this world. We are, sadly so, storing our treasure where moths and rust are certain to destroy it. We disregard, on a daily basis, Christ's admonition to be like the lilies of the field and neither toil nor spin for material things.

A Theology of Happiness

Unfortunately, many modern Christians have gone the way of the world and adopted Madison Avenue values. This is what a popular senior pastor of one of the largest churches in America writes:

Maybe you have come from a poor environment, or maybe you don't have a lot of material possessions right now. That's okay; God has good things ahead for you. But let me caution you; don't allow that poverty image to become ingrained inside you. Don't grow accustomed to living with less, doing less, and being less to the point that you eventually sit back and accept it. "We've always been poor. This is the way it's got to be."

No, start looking through eyes of faith, seeing yourself rising to new levels. See yourself prospering, and keep that image in your heart and mind. You may be living in poverty at the moment, but don't ever let poverty live in you.

This same pastor assures people, "Your lot in life is to continually increase. Your lot in life is to be an overcomer, to live prosperously in every area." And as one televangelist exclaims: "If my heart really, honestly desires a nice Cadillac...would there be something terribly wrong with me saying, 'Lord, it is the desire of my heart to have a nice car...and I'll use it for Your glory'?"

To many, this may sound great—but only if heard through ears that have become so accustomed to preaching which convinces us that God's will invariably involves endless material blessings, the kind of blessings that are valued in this world—material wealth, happiness in our relationships with others, success in our businesses.

This is the modern American notion of the prosperity theology, which stresses material riches as a goal of life. But did Jesus Christ enjoy an abundance of the things this world has to offer? Did His disciples? No. They eschewed materialism. Their lives were difficult. They endured persecution and great hardship. They were hated by the world because they were not of the world.

The prosperity gospel is littered with pastors and motivational speakers who not only promote becoming rich, they are rich themselves. But according to the Gospels, Christ preferred the company of the lowly and despised to that of the rich and powerful. And He crossed lines of ritual purification to help the unclean—lepers, the possessed, the insane, prostitutes, adulterers and collaborators with the tyrannical occupying empire, Rome.

Christ, as a cabinetmaker's son, had a lower-class upbringing. "That was a trade usually marginal and itinerant in his time," notes Gary Wills in *What Christ Meant*. "He chose his followers from the lower class, from fishermen, dependent on the season's catch, or from a despised trade (tax collection for the Romans). There were no Scribes or scholars of the Law in his following."

Jesus not only favored the homeless, He was himself homeless during His public life. "Foxes have holes and birds of the air *have* nests," Christ proclaims, "but the Son of Man has nowhere to lay *His* head." As a consequence, Jesus depended on others to shelter Him. He especially depended on women, who were considered second-class citizens in His culture, for assistance.

Clearly, the prosperity gospel is a Christianity in crisis for the simple reason that it has absorbed the two prominent values of modern materialistic society: personal peace and affluence. But in the true sense of the word, these do not really deserve the name "values." As Francis Schaeffer writes in *The Church at the End of the 20th Century*: "Affluence and personal peace at any price as the controlling factors of life are as ugly as anything can be." And, eventually, even those who call themselves Christians will distort their true purpose in life and turn into manipulators of others to maintain these so-called "values."

This manipulation often comes in the form of the

new age concept of "empowerment" that has infiltrated many modern churches. "As a precedent we have the serpent who 'empowered' Adam and Eve," writes Garret Keizer in *Help: The Original Human Dilemma*. "Empowerment as it's often practiced is nothing more than fleecing sheep with the help of a motivational speaker."

Had Dietrich Bonhoeffer's concern been with his own empowerment, personal peace or "success," he surely would have remained safely in America or in England when the war began. And no one would have faulted him for doing so. An influential theologian, he could have safely lived out his years preaching and teaching God's Word and gaining great respect from all who heard him, as well as considerable material comforts.

But his primary concern was not for a life of success—even a life of what others would have considered a successful *ministry*. No. His primary concern was to be like Christ. For him, that meant helping people in a practical way, just as Jesus did. It meant speaking Truth to power. And it meant returning to his country to be with those most desperate for his help, although that choice meant certain hardship, suffering and even death for Bonhoeffer.

Thus, Bonhoeffer disregarded not only success but even personal well-being. Because he understood that just as our purpose in life is not to be "successful" or prosperous in the sense of securing a powerful place in society or amassing worldly goods, so our purpose in life is not to be "happy." As Bonhoeffer said, "personal suffering has become a more useful key for understanding the world than personal happiness."

This is not to say that owning a nice home or a decent car or having money in the bank is non-Christian. To the contrary. But it is our duty to use our God-given resources to reach out and help those in need. Such is the essential reason for possessing wealth. As Christ tells us, it is not money itself but the *love* of money that is the root of all evil.

However, even many who understand that material goods should not be their focus often devote their lives to pursuing more abstract, worldly pleasures. We might turn to our relationships with our spouses and children, seeking and expecting our fulfillment in life to come from them. Or we might look to a pattern of personal growth and achievements as a source of confidence and happiness. Or we might seek empowerment. Or we might seek to find "peace within ourselves" to feel more at ease with our pursuits in life.

Ministers or leaders who urge us in these directions, however, are only saying what the surrounding secular consensus is saying, but in theological terms. They leave us with only contentless "god words," as they have cut themselves from the true meaning of Jesus Christ.

Regardless of whether we look for things to bring us happiness or whether we seek our fulfillment in these more abstract ways, we are simply seeking the wrong thing. Yet swarms of Christians who are steeped in the church—even those who are faithful to spending time in daily devotionals and learning the Bible inside and out—have convinced themselves that a God who loves them must surely mean for them to be "happy." Unfortunately, this faulty theology of happiness is an illusion. It has had devastating effects on the individual lives of those who embrace it and on the body of Christ as a whole.

When we take the theology of happiness to its logical conclusion, we find that it results in our recreating a god in *our* image; a god who suits our whims; a god whose definition of right and wrong fits neatly within our own; a god who wouldn't ask anything of us that is too difficult, let alone painful. In other words, we are worshipping idols created from our own minds.

CHAPTER SEVEN

Suffering Is Unavoidable

When I lay these questions before God I get no answer. But a rather special sort of "No Answer." It is not the locked door. It is more like a silent, certainly not uncompassionate, gaze. As though He shook His head not in refusal but waiving the question. Like, "Peace, child; you don't understand."

—C. S. Lewis,
A Grief Observed

How do we explain suffering and pain? How do we explain the suffering and pain that are inevitable if we are to serve Christ? And why are suffering and pain, most often inflicted by human beings on other human beings, so widespread?

True Christianity explains the nature and behavior of people, the world and the suffering around us in terms of the flaws caused by the historic, space-time Fall. The Fall proceeded from an act of willing disobedience. By bestowing free will on man, God exalted human beings. Thus, God did not create robots but creatures of significance whose choices affect not only themselves but those around them as well. And inherent in the gift of free will was the right to choose between good and evil. The latter was chosen. As a consequence, the Fall brought depravity to all facets of the human being and blighted nature as well—explaining most of the cataclysmic environmental events such as earthquakes, hurricanes and the like. Moreover, the effects of the Fall are pervasive and are inherent to every member of the human race.

Despite the often chaotic nature of existence, many modern philosophers, in rejecting the Fall, assert that people are inherently good. However, they have no real answer to the fact that the supposedly noble attributes of people are marred by selfishness, vice and cruelty. Such philosophers view God as pure benevolence or a kind of "Life Force." However, this is not the God revealed in either the Old or New Testament. As Richard Lovelace explains in *The Dynamics of Spiritual Life*:

The tension between God's holy righteousness and his compassionate mercy cannot be legitimately resolved by remolding his character into an image of pure benevolence as the church did in the nineteenth century. There is only one way that this contradiction can be removed: through the cross of Christ which reveals the severity of God's anger through the vicarious sacrifice of his Son. In systems which resolve this tension by softening the character of God, Christ and his work become an addendum, and spiritual darkness becomes complete because the true God has been abandoned for the worship of a magnified image of human tolerance.

Clearly, a denial of the Fall and the proposition that man is inherently good and what we see in nature is normal presents a dilemma. The view that there is no abnormality in nature is a very practical problem and was addressed by renowned writer and existentialist Albert Camus in his novel *The Plague*. Camus comments on the predicament facing Orion the ratcatcher: "Well, if he joins with the doctors and fights the plague, he is fighting against God, or if he joins with the priest and does not fight God by not fighting the plague, he is not being humanitarian." Camus never resolved this problem in either his literature or his life.

If what *is* is normal, then how does one explain nature when it is destructive? Is there an answer? Can I fight a plague and not fight God?

The Christian can fight it. As Francis

Schaeffer argues in *Pollution and the Death of Man*, when Christ stood in front of the tomb of Lazarus, He was claiming to be divine and yet He was furious. Christ "could be furious with the plague *without being angry with Himself*. This turns upon the historic, space-time Fall." Consequently, the Christian does not have the difficulty faced in Camus' predicament.

Christianity, as such, provides the restoration to the Fall in the atoning work of Jesus Christ on the cross. Because of Christ's willing sacrifice for humankind, God grants full forgiveness to those who by faith accept Jesus Christ's redemptive work. This does not mean that those who believe are thereby perfect. To put it in medical terms, the fatal infection of sin is cured through Christ's work on the cross, but the symptoms remain. The believer is, therefore, substantially healed by Christ's work, but he or she is never perfect in this life. Through Christ's voluntary death for our sins, however, God's justice and love are reconciled and the way of salvation is open for those who accept the gift of God through faith in Jesus Christ.

But because the symptoms of the Fall are still with us, suffering and pain will continue. Therefore, we need to acknowledge the tragedy of life but hopefully work to heal it.

Moreover, suffering is not an optional choice in the faith but rather an essential aspect of true Christianity. For Christians, suffering for what is right is never meaningless. Indeed, Christ uses suffering as a way to mature and perfect the believer. As the Apostle Paul notes in Hebrews: "In bringing many sons to the glory, it was fitting that God, for whom and through whom everything exists, should make the author of their salvation perfect through suffering." How then should the followers of Christ escape the need for a similar process?

A Good God

The existence of suffering does not mean that we are not dealing with a good God. Quite the opposite is true.

Before going any further, we must be honest in saying that our conception of good differs from that of God. There are those who argue that a good God would permit no suffering at all. But this is an anthropomorphic view of God that does not square with the Bible.

Then there are times when we all question why we suffer. Sometimes we blame God. But God does not experiment with our faith or our lives in order to find out their quality. He already knows that the temples we build are a house of cards. And His only way of making us realize this fact is to knock them down.

Therefore, we must cast away our foolish pride and begin from the premise that we are fallen and depraved. "We are so depraved," writes C. S. Lewis in *A Grief Observed*,

> that our ideas of goodness count for nothing; or worse than nothing—the very fact that we think something is good is presumptive evidence that it is really bad. Now God has in fact—our worst fears are true—all the characteristics we regard as bad: unreasonableness, vanity, vindictiveness, injustice, cruelty. But all these

blacks (as they seem to us) are really whites. It's only our depravity that makes them look black to us.

As difficult as it is to understand, a good God who created a good world gave human beings an awesome gift—free will—to do with as we wanted. And by a free will act of disobedience by His creatures—a disobedience which continues to this day—all the pain and suffering we see in our torn, ruptured world is the result. "Suffering, destruction, disease, and death itself are, therefore, ultimately traceable to the freely sinful human will as a condition that is, strictly speaking, *un*natural," Ellis Sandoz writes in his book *Political Apocalypse*. "For by nature all that is *is* good, as coming from the hand of God. Even the demons *are* not devoid of goodness: inasmuch as they are (rather than are not), they partake of Being and goodness."

However, when people become depraved through sin, it does not simply affect them. Instead, they hurt one another as well. Such hurtful acts of people against people account for four-fifths of the sufferings of humanity. "It is men, not God, who have produced racks, whips, prisons, slavery, guns, bayonets, and bombs," writes C. S. Lewis in *The Problem of Pain*. Instead, "it is by human avarice or human stupidity, not by the churlishness of nature, that we have poverty and overwork."

The problem of pain and suffering through persecution of Christians in particular is evident in countries around the world. Such is not true generally of Christians in the West. For example, Christians in the United States suffer much less persecution than Christians in other parts of the world. As a consequence, they do not compare well with the first Christians or with those solitary souls who die or are killed because they are believers who will not be silenced.

For example, some Christians in America have told me that they would not fight for their freedom to speak about their faith because they might lose their jobs. In such instances, discomfort becomes the measure of how far one will go to stand up for the truth. The striving for happiness, personal peace and affluence is more important than practicing true Christianity.

In the process of avoiding the duty to stand and be counted, modern evangelicalism tends to twist the "goodness" of God into "lovingness." "And by Love, in this context, most of us mean kindness—the desire to see others than the self happy; not happy in this way or in that, but just happy," notes C. S. Lewis. He continues:

> What would really satisfy us would be a God who said of anything we happened to like doing, "What does it matter so long as they are contented?" We want, in fact, not so much a Father in Heaven as a grandfather in heaven—a senile benevolence who, as they say, "liked to see young people enjoying themselves" and whose plan for the universe was simply that it might be truly said at the end of the day, "a good time was had by all."

CHAPTER EIGHT

Deny Yourself, Take Up the Cross, Follow Him

I will have no right to participate in the reconstruction of Christian life in Germany after the war if I do not share the trials of this time with my people.... Christians in Germany will face the terrible alternative of either willing the defeat of their nation in order that Christian civilization might survive, or willing the victory of their nation and thereby destroying our civilization. I know which of these alternatives I must choose; but I cannot make that choice in the security of America.

—Dietrich Bonhoeffer

We must through many tribulations enter the kingdom of God.

—The Apostle Paul

Accoording to Christ, anyone who wishes to be His disciple must do three things: deny himself, take up his cross and follow Him.

Self-Denial

What does it mean to deny ourselves? We tend to think of the command in terms of letting go of our material possessions, and that certainly can be an element of it. But the Greek word here is the one we would use for "disown." In fact, it is the same word used when Peter disowns Christ after being accused of being a disciple.

Renowned minister Ray C. Stedman explained self-disowning: "Denying self means that we repudiate our natural feelings about ourselves, i.e., our right to ourselves, our right to run our own lives. We are to deny that we own ourselves. We do not have the final right to decide what we are going to do, or where we are going to go. When it is stated in those terms, people sense immediately that Jesus is saying something very fundamental. It strikes right at the heart of our very existence, because the one thing that we, as human beings, value and covet and protect above anything else is the right to make ultimate decisions for ourselves. We refuse to be under anything or anybody, but reserve the right to make the final decisions of our lives. This is what Jesus is talking about…. If you are going to follow Jesus, you no longer own yourself. He has ultimate rights; he has Lordship of your life."

As Stedman indicates, denying ourselves is not easy to do. Many Christians who refer to Jesus as "Lord" have never actually taken the step of giving up the throne of their lives. Our default mode is to go about our day-to-day lives pursuing our own goals and objectives, our own happiness.

Taking Up the Cross

Yet true self-denial is absolutely necessary for the one who is bent on becoming a disciple of Jesus. And it is only the first step, a prerequisite for the next step, which is to "take up our cross." The very idea of taking up a cross, when seriously considered, is enough to strike terror in the heart of even the most determined would-be disciple among us. But once we have truly denied ourselves by losing our awareness of self and the difficult road before us, taking up our cross becomes possible.

In Dietrich Bonhoeffer's book *The Cost of Discipleship*, he explores what it means to take up one's cross and begin discipleship:

> The cross means sharing the suffering of Christ to the last and to the fullest…. The cross is there, right from the beginning, [the person] has only got to pick it up: there is no need for him to go out and look for a cross for himself, no need for him to deliberately run after suffering. Jesus says that every Christian has his own cross waiting for him, a cross destined and appointed by God. Each must endure his allotted share of suffering and rejection…. But it is one and the same cross in every case. The cross is laid on every Christian.

Bonhoeffer certainly practiced what he preached. Each of us should ask ourselves, "Have I willingly taken up my cross in order to follow Jesus, or do I go about my days seeking to minimize my own discomforts and maximize my enjoyment of this world and the things it has to offer?" Do we respond willingly and obediently when God puts hardships in our paths, or do we grumble and complain like the Israelites who were so quick to forget the God who had rescued them from slavery?

Often, because practicing true Christianity is difficult, many seek the avenue of least resistance. As C.S. Lewis recognized, true Christianity has not been tried and found wanting but rather found difficult and not tried.

Jesus explained to His original disciples that, for them, suffering was not just a possibility—it was inevitable. In John 15:20, He makes this very clear: "A servant is not greater than his master. If they persecuted Me, they will also persecute you." And, indeed, those original disciples faced persecution in the most extreme forms. Matthew was slain by a sword at a distant city in

Ethiopia. Mark was dragged through the streets of Alexandria. Luke was hanged on an olive tree in Greece. John was put in a pot of boiling oil but miraculously escaped and was later exiled to Patmos. Peter was crucified in Rome with his head downward. James, the Greater, was beheaded in Jerusalem. James, the Lesser, was thrown from the Temple and then beaten to death with a club. Bartholomew was whipped to death. Andrew was bound to a cross, from which he continued to preach to his persecutors until he died. Thomas was lanced in the East Indies. Jude was shot to death with arrows. They all departed this world as victors, as friends of Jesus, because they refused to become aligned with the world.

The cross, therefore, is not the terrible end to an otherwise happy life. And bearing a cross is not simply something that happened to first-generation disciples. In fact, it meets us all at the beginning of our relationship with Christ. It is not likely that many of us will be martyred for our faith. Nonetheless, Christ has assured us that if we are His disciples, we will have a cross to bear in this world. Bonhoeffer summed it up this way: "When Christ calls a man, he bids him come and die."

Our dying to the world and our natural habits and desires begins from the moment we count the cost and heed the call of Jesus. We must, at once, put to death any desire or habit that threatens our allegiance to God or conflicts with His moral demands.

For the rich young ruler, it meant giving all his possessions to the poor. For the husband who is not meeting his wife's emotional needs, it means striving to follow the admonition to love his wife as Christ loved His church—in other words, a willingness to sacrifice all for her, including all worldly pursuits. For the wife, it means determining every day to strive to respect her husband in word and deed. For the one who has been deeply hurt by another, it means extending true forgiveness to the offender. For all of us, it means giving of our time and resources to care for the poor, the sick and the hurting of this world. But be warned: it is only possible for us to carry these crosses as we cling to Jesus and focus not on ourselves but single-mindedly on Him and His grace, which are sufficient for us.

To quote Bonhoeffer again, "Just as Christ is Christ only in virtue of his suffering and rejection, so the disciple is a disciple only in so far as he shares his Lord's suffering and rejection and crucifixion. Discipleship means adherence to the person of Jesus, and therefore submission to the law of Christ which is the law of the cross."

Following Christ

Once we have denied ourselves and taken up our cross, Jesus bids us to follow Him. He doesn't give us a roadmap or an itinerary but simply commands, "Follow Me!" Isn't it incredible that although this call appears to be devoid of all content, the original disciples did not balk or ask questions. They simply followed. They left all they had: family, friends, careers, possessions. They followed because they recognized the inherent value of the One who had called them.

Thus, everything else in life becomes absolutely insignificant to the man or woman who heeds the call to follow Christ. This is the true meaning of faith. "Faith can no longer mean sitting still and waiting—they must rise and follow him," writes Bonhoeffer. "The call frees them from all earthly ties, and binds them to Jesus Christ alone. They must burn their boats and plunge into absolute insecurity in order to learn the demand and the gift of Christ."

In the book of Luke, we are told of a few would-be disciples who are too closely bound to their own lives and positions in the world to heed the call. One of them wants to bury his father before he begins discipleship. Jesus says, "Let the dead bury their own dead." Another man wants to say goodbye to his family before setting off on this uncertain journey. Jesus responds that, "No one, having put his hand to the plow, and looking back, is fit for the kingdom of God."

The disciple may not make excuses. He may not dictate his own terms for the relationship. *He is called simply to follow*. And these verses make it clear that following Jesus means cutting ourselves off from our prior existence in a very real way.

Another thing is clear as well: no man can choose such a life for himself. As Bonhoeffer recognized: "No man can call himself to such a destiny, says Jesus, and his word stays unanswered. The gulf between a voluntary offer to follow and genuine discipleship is clear. But where Jesus calls, he bridges the widest gulf."

Cast Away

In the movie *Cast Away*, there is a scene in which Tom Hanks, stranded alone on a secluded island, loses Wilson—the "companion" he created from a volleyball that had washed up on the shore. He paints a face on Wilson and talks to "him," which seems to be the only thing that allows Hanks to maintain a thread of sanity. Eventually, Hanks' character builds a makeshift raft, on which he pins all his hopes of returning to civilization, and sets off with Wilson.

While he is sleeping, a huge storm comes up. And just before Hanks wakes up, Wilson becomes dislodged and begins to drift away in the ocean. When Hanks realizes that his companion is missing, he screams frantically for him. Desperate, he jumps off the raft and swims, screaming, toward the place where Wilson is drifting. But he realizes his raft is drifting in the opposite direction and starts paddling back to avoid losing it. Then comes the crucial moment when, halfway between Wilson and the raft, Hanks realizes that he cannot have both.

He could recapture Wilson and cling to the companion he had known for so long, but he would die. He chooses to swim back to his raft because he knows that only the raft can save him from his plight.

This is a dim picture of how Christians should cling to Christ, leaving behind, whenever necessary, our familiar comforts and every vestige of the life that would pull our attention or our commitment away from Him. We must shun the materialistic focus of this world and live as pilgrims, understanding that we are not citizens of this world. We are not here to accumulate wealth and seek pleasure. Those things are like worthless "Wilsons" that will soon pass away. Instead, we should spend our time trying to rescue others who, like us, have eternal souls within them. We must show them how the raft we have found—Jesus Christ—can save them as well.

This requires the disciple of Christ to take a very definite step where only true faith is possible. What does this mean? It means that we can only take the crucial step of faith when we fix our eyes not on ourselves, but on the word with which Jesus calls us. In Matthew 14, Peter knew that he dare not climb out of the ship on his own strength. In fact, his very first step would be his undoing. And so Peter cries, "Lord, if it is You, command me to come to You on the water." And Jesus answers: "Come."

It was Peter's step of obedience that was taken before his faith was possible. Unless he obeyed, he could not believe.

CHAPTER NINE

Speak Truth to Power

The world expects of Christians that they
will raise their voices so loudly and clearly and so formulate their protest that not
even the simplest man can have the
slightest doubt about what they are saying. Further, the world expects of
Christians that they will eschew all fuzzy
abstractions and plant themselves
squarely in front of the bloody face of history. We stand in need of folk who have
determined to speak directly and unmis-
takably and come what may, to stand by
what they have said.
                    —Albert Camus

Truth is precisely what true Christianity has to offer. Curiously, it is sometimes the non-Christian who sees the need to stand for truth. For example, French existentialist Albert Camus claimed to believe in nothing and to consider everything absurd. But Camus was able to see the needs of the age in a way matched by few of his peers.

Notice that there is no doubt in his mind that Christianity is inherently *opposed* to the spirit of the age, or what he calls the "bloody face of history." By his standard, the posture of compromise or a noncommittal attitude is fatal. Camus expected Christians to spurn abstractions and hold clear, well-defined beliefs. He said they must not only raise their voices, but do so loudly and in such a way that there is no doubt as to what is being said. That done, they must stand by what they have said. One could hardly put it any better.

Hot or Cold

Sadly, in many instances we are left with a

diluted Christianity that lacks the strength to speak truth to a torn world. Above all, it is a gospel virtually devoid of spiritual content.

Francis Schaeffer distinguished between the hot (high content) communication and cool (low content) communication that he saw developing as early as the 1970s. However, this distinction is even more apropos today. As Schaeffer wrote in his book *The Church at the End of the Twentieth Century*, if one wants to sell a product, he or she will not use hot communication for the simple reason that communication with content—moral right and wrong, for example—tends to offend:

> In other words, when people have been trained to respond like a salivating dog to the ringing of a bell, you must not try to feed things through reason. It will not work. I would reverse this. In a day of increasing cool communication, biblical Christianity must make very plain that it will deal only with hot communication. Biblical Christianity rests upon content, factual content. It does not cause people

to react merely emotionally in a first-order experience.

Furthermore, Schaeffer notes:

Every single preaching of the gospel must be related to strong content. We must not fall into the cheap solution of beginning to use these cool means of communication and cause people to seem to make professions of faith. If we fall into this kind of manipulation, we have cut Christianity down to the ground because we are only adding to the loss of the appropriate control which reason should have. We are throwing ourselves wide open to future problems. Christianity must fight for its life to insist that it deals with content—content which stands in contrast to that which is not true.

There is another way—one devoted to the same self-sacrifice that the teachings of Christ demand. For example, Philip Yancey tells of an experience he had one summer when he met with a group of Wycliffe Bible translators at their austere headquarters in the Arizona desert. Their meetings transpired in a concrete-block building with a metal roof, and many of them lived in mobile homes. These talented linguists were preparing to go to the far corners of the world to live a life of poverty. But they recognized that someday, though probably not in this lifetime, God would richly reward their sacrifice. Yancey recounts how one morning, as he was jogging nearby, he came across a massive, shimmering resort, complete with two Olympic swimming pools, aerobic workout rooms, lush gardens and horse stables. These facilities belonged to a famous eating disorder clinic that catered to movie stars and athletes. It struck Yancey that while one institution endeavored to save souls and prepare people to serve, the other endeavored to save bodies, to prepare people to enjoy this life.

This is precisely what Christ is referring to in Matthew 6:24 when He proclaims that one cannot "serve God and mammon." Mammon—materiality, riches, excessive personal pursuits—all require sacrifice, specifically to the god of self.

Persevere

I know the picture of discipleship I've painted seems very difficult and somewhat dismal. But the simple truth is that for discipleship, there is a price. And it is costly and painful. As Bonhoeffer writes in *The Cost of Discipleship*:

> The messengers of Jesus will be hated to the end of time. They will be blamed for all the divisions which rend cities and homes. Jesus and his disciples will be condemned on all sides for undermining family life, and for leading the nation astray; they will be called crazy fanatics and disturbers of the peace. The disciples will be sorely tempted to desert their Lord. But the end is also near, and they must hold on and persevere until it comes. Only he will

be blessed who remains loyal to Jesus and his word until the end.

Of course, this does not mean that Christians should fall into the self-righteous trap of the persecution complex. It simply means that practicing true Christianity will necessarily result in suffering.

Serving Christ means focusing on helping others—the downtrodden, the sick, the wretched, the wronged, the outcast and all who are tortured with guilt and anxiety—and consorting with sinners and enemies, even if it means being treated as an outcast yourself. We often forget that Christ died on the cross alone, abandoned even by His disciples. "With him were crucified, not two of his followers, but two murderers," writes Bonhoeffer. "But they all stood beneath the cross, enemies and believers, doubters and cowards, revilers and devoted followers. His prayer, in that hour, and his forgiveness, was meant for them all, and for all their sins. The mercy and love of God are at work even in the midst of his enemies."

Serving Christ also means eschewing materialism and standing against the flow. If you do, you will be persecuted. It could be financial, physical or mental persecution, and it will be very difficult. As Christ said in Matthew 10: "And you will be hated by all for My name's sake." In obedience, however, there is a promise: "But he who endures to the end will be saved."

One thing is certain. For the Christian, suffering is not an optional choice in faith. Rather, as Christ specifically noted, suffering and persecution would follow. But there is hope: "In the world you will have tribulation; but be of good cheer, I have overcome the world."